Dear Parents and Educators,

W9-CLW-675

Welcome to Penguin Young Readers! As parents and educators, you know that each child develops at their own pace—in terms of speech, critical thinking, and, of course, reading. Penguin Young Readers recognizes this fact. As a result, each Penguin Young Readers book is assigned a traditional easy-to-read level (1–4) as well as an F&P Text Level (A–R). Both of these systems will help you choose the right book for your child. Please refer to the back of each book for specific leveling information. Penguin Young Readers features esteemed authors and illustrators, stories about favorite characters, fascinating nonfiction, and more!

Are Dragons Real?

LEVEL 4

F&P TEXT LEVEL R

This book is perfect for a **Fluent Reader** who:
- can read the text quickly with minimal effort;
- has good comprehension skills;
- can self-correct (can recognize when something doesn't sound right); and
- can read aloud smoothly and with expression.

Here are some **activities** you can do during and after reading this book:
- Comprehension: After reading the book, answer the following questions:
  - How long ago did the oldest dragon stories begin being told, and in what country?
  - What country has a red dragon on its flag?
  - Which animal is described as the "most fearsome lizard alive," and what makes its bite so dangerous?
- Nonfiction: Nonfiction books deal with facts and events that are real. Talk about the elements of nonfiction. Discuss some of the facts you learned about dragons. Then, on a separate sheet of paper, write down facts about your favorite dragons from this book.

Remember, sharing the love of reading with a child is the best gift you can give!

*This book has been officially leveled by using the F&P Text Level Gradient™ leveling system.

For all who believe in magic—GLC

PENGUIN YOUNG READERS

An Imprint of Penguin Random House LLC, New York

Penguin supports copyright. Copyright fuels creativity, encourages diverse voices, promotes free speech, and creates a vibrant culture. Thank you for buying an authorized edition of this book and for complying with copyright laws by not reproducing, scanning, or distributing any part of it in any form without permission. You are supporting writers and allowing Penguin to continue to publish books for every reader.

Photo credits: used throughout: (frames) subjug/E+/Getty Images; cover, 3: © Direk Tomyim/ 123RF.COM; 4: Vac1/iStock/Getty Images; 5: sharifphoto/iStock/Getty Images; 6–7: Videowok_art/ iStock/Getty Images; 8–9: Liufuyu/iStock/Getty Images; 10: (Dragon Robe, Bequest of Mrs. James W. Gerard, 1956) public domain, via the Metropolitan Museum of Art (CC0 1.0); 11: 123Nelson/ Shutterstock.com; 12, 13: Album/British Library/Alamy Stock Photo; 14: (top) duncan1890/ DigitalVision Vectors/Getty Images; 14–15: Lebrecht Music & Arts/Alamy Stock Photo; 15: (The Dragon of India from *Cosmographia* [1544] by Sebastian Münster) public domain, via Wikimedia Commons; 16: Werner Forman Archive/Universitetets Oldsaksamling, Oslo/Heritage Images/Heritage Image Partnership Ltd/Alamy Stock Photo; 17: (from *Stories of Beowulf* [1908] by Henrietta Elizabeth Marshall) public domain, via Wikimedia Commons; 18: Art Collection 4/Alamy Stock Photo; 19: Jorge Láscar, via Wikimedia Commons (CC BY 2.0); 20: Art Collection 2/Alamy Stock Photo; 21: Aetheling1125 at English Wikipedia, via Wikimedia Commons (CC BY-SA 3.0); 22: csfotoimages/iStock/Getty Images; 23: RudolfT/iStock/Getty Images; 24: Universal Images Group North America LLC/De Agostini Picture Library/Alamy Stock Photo; 25: ANDREYGUDKOV/iStock/Getty Images; 26: photosbyash/iStock/ Getty Images; 27: MindStorm-inc/iStock/Getty Images; 28: Jean-Paul Ferrero/AUSCAPE/Auscape International Pty Ltd/Alamy Stock Photo; 29: warren farnell/iStock/Getty Images; 30: Howard Chen/ iStock/Getty Images; 31: TatianaMironenko/iStock/Getty Images; 32: johan63/iStock/Getty Images; 33: zhnger/iStock/Getty Images; 34: Michael Loccisano/Getty Images Entertainment/Getty Images; 35: Digital Vision/DigitalVision/Getty Images; 36: (top) Valter Jacinto/Moment/Getty Images, (bottom) Windmill Books/Universal Images Group North America LLC/Alamy Stock Photo; 37: Clarisse Cespedes/iStock/Getty Images; 38: freeman98589/iStock/Getty Images; 39: S.Rohrlach/iStock/ Getty Images; 40: Nuttanin Kanakornboonyawat/Alamy Stock Photo; 41: volkerpreusser/Alamy Stock Photo; 42: Egmont Strigl/Getty Images; 43: Madeleine_Steinbach/iStock/Getty Images; 44: Bofot/ iStock/Getty Images; 45: R.M. Nunes/iStock/Getty Images; 46: (detail from Asia on the Hunt-Lenox Globe [1510]) public domain, via The New York Public Library (CC0 1.0); 47: (top and bottom) angelinast/iStock/Getty Images; 48: Paula Montenegro/Alamy Stock Photo

Text copyright © 2021 by Ginjer L. Clarke. All rights reserved.
Published by Penguin Young Readers, an imprint of Penguin Random House LLC, New York.
Manufactured in China.

Visit us online at www.penguinrandomhouse.com.

Library of Congress Cataloging-in-Publication Data is available upon request.

ISBN 9780593093160 (pbk)   10 9 8 7 6 5 4 3 2 1
ISBN 9780593093177 (hc)   10 9 8 7 6 5 4 3 2 1

ARE DRAGONS REAL?

by Ginjer L. Clarke

What Is a Dragon?

A dragon was believed to be a winged creature that breathed fire and lived in a cave. The Greek word *draken* meant "to watch." Dragons were seen as guards who watched over treasure.

But the Latin word *draco* meant "huge serpent," or a large snake. Some people believed dragons were snake-like creatures that could swim—both in water and in air.

In Western nations such as England and Scotland, people described dragons as scary, scaly monsters. And they feared that dragons ate people. Yikes!

But in Asian countries such as China and Japan, people believed dragons were smart serpents with beards and antlers. And these dragons brought people good luck.

Where did the ideas of such different dragons come from?

Dragon Stories
and Art

Tales of dragons have been told for a very long time, all around the world. The oldest dragon stories began in China and other parts of Asia about 5,000 years ago.

Many people thought dragons controlled the weather. These dragons slept quietly in the oceans in winter. *Whoosh!* Then they flew into the air in spring, creating thunder and rain. The dragons could change size to be as small as a cup or as big as the sky.

The Nine Dragon Wall
in Beijing, China

Dragons were so important in ancient China that the emperor was called the "True Dragon." He wore fancy robes with dragon images sewn into them.

Many Chinese people today still feel that dragons are lucky. A dragon dance is performed to celebrate the Lunar New Year. Dancers hold up a long, colorful dragon puppet on wooden poles.

Bam! Bam! They move the dragon together—up, down, and all around—to the music of drummers. The longer the dragon, the more luck for all people.

An ancient Roman author named Pliny (say: PLIN-ee) the Elder wrote a book almost 2,000 years ago after he traveled to India. He described animals he said he had seen, including some he believed to be dragons and unicorns.

Pliny wrote that a dragon could wrap itself around an elephant, kill it, and drink its blood! This "dragon" was likely just a giant python snake, which squeezes its prey to death.

Another type of book that described animals that people believed were real was called a bestiary (say: BES-chee-eh-ree)—from the Latin for "beast." These books also included dragons.

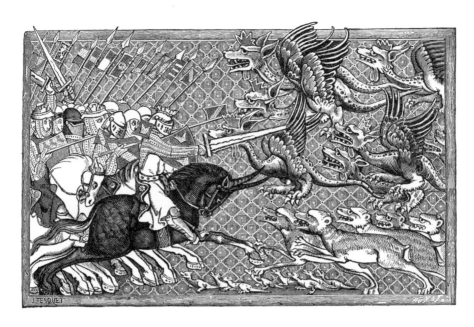

Alexander the Great
from ancient Greece
also traveled to India
and told stories of
dragons. Alexander
reported that he saw
a serpent with wings
hiding in a cave—
and battled it!

Other writers and
explorers, including

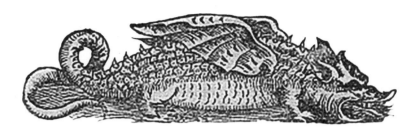

Marco Polo, also described seeing huge, frightening serpents.

Many years later, people wrote stories about dragons that were based on these earlier tales. But now their stories told of dragons as giant flying lizards!

Fighting Dragons

Most dragon stories have one thing in common—a brave dragon slayer.

An ancient tale from Iceland tells of a terrible dragon that breathed poison and stole some gold. A bold warrior named Sigurd stabbed the dragon with his sword and took the treasure.

The oldest known written story of a dragon slayer is called *Beowulf.* A dragon becomes angry when someone steals its treasure, so it burns a town. Beowulf bravely fights the dragon, but it bites him. His friend helps him kill the dragon. The people of the town are saved, but Beowulf dies.

The most famous story of a dragon slayer is Saint George. He was thought to be an English knight who lived during the Middle Ages. A fierce dragon was destroying a town. The king's daughter was about to be killed. *Oh no!*

Suddenly, the fearless George charges in on his white horse. He stabs the dragon under the wing and saves the princess. *Hurray!*

Another story from the Middle Ages
is about Merlin the magician and King
Vortigern. Merlin told the king that two
dragons—one white and one red—lived
under the mountain where the king was
building a castle.

Roar! The dragons kept fighting and cracking the castle, until the king's men freed them. The white dragon fled, but the red dragon stayed to defend the castle.

This castle was real, and the ruins of it have been found on a hilltop in Wales called Dinas Emrys. Wow!

The red dragon became a symbol of courage for the people of Wales. The red dragon is even on the flag of Wales. Cool!

Dragons are also seen on many coats of arms—images that represent a family or country. Flags with the coat of arms were carried into battle so knights on the same side could find each other. Dragons on the coat of arms were a symbol of the knights' bravery.

Real-Life Dragons

Megalania was the largest kind of lizard ever. It probably inspired many tales of dragons. *Megalania* lived thousands of years ago. It grew up to about 25 feet long, and it weighed over 1,000 pounds—more than a polar bear!

Do dragons still roam the earth?
Yes! The Komodo dragon is the most
fearsome lizard alive, as well as the
heaviest. It cannot breathe fire, but it
does have a venomous bite. *Chomp!* The
dragon bites its prey. The venom poisons
the animal, which then dies slowly.

The smaller Australian bearded dragon also has venom in its bite. *Hiss!* The bearded dragon tries to look big and fierce. It shows its teeth, puffs out its throat, and shakes the black spikes on its beard.

Not all dragons are dangerous. The Chinese water dragon is friendly and gentle. *Hello!* It bobs its head and waves its front arms to communicate with other water dragons.

The tiny Asian flying dragon can really fly, almost like in the stories of dragons. The flying dragon spreads the colorful skin flaps along its body. *Whee!* It can glide over 100 feet between trees. It uses its tail to change direction.

The Australian frilled dragon has skin flaps, too, but around its neck. *Pop!* The frilled dragon expands its frill—like an umbrella—to look bigger and more fearsome to an enemy.

The leafy sea dragon looks like an imaginary serpent with its curvy body and fancy fins. The tiny sea dragon uses its camouflage (say: KAH-muh-flazh) to blend perfectly into the seaweed.

The dragon moray eel is a monster of the sea. *Crunch!* It eats almost anything it can fit into its mouth. And it has two sets of teeth—one for catching its prey and another for swallowing it.

Wannabe Dragons

The enormous Nile crocodile could easily be mistaken for a dragon. Its giant lizard body and long scaly tail make it seem like a dragon without wings. This crocodile is also a fierce fighter, as dragons were believed to be.

The Chinese alligator may have inspired the tale of the wise Chinese dragon. Alligators are water creatures, they are good problem solvers, and they can live a long time—just like the dragons in Chinese stories.

Titanoboa was an enormous snake that lived millions of years ago. This 40-foot-long serpent could be the real animal that inspired stories of ancient sea dragons. Anacondas are the largest snakes alive now, and they are related to *Titanoboa.*

The spitting cobra is very dangerous. It does not breathe fire. But it can spray venom—up to six feet away! Worst of all, the cobra aims for its victim's eyes, which causes burning pain and blindness. Ouch!

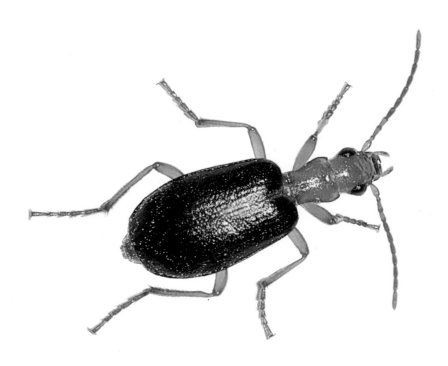

The bombardier beetle may not look like a dragon, but it can almost spit fire! *Bombardier* (say: bom-buh-DEER) means "one who releases bombs." This beetle mixes chemicals inside its body. *Boom!* The boiling-hot liquid explodes out of its body and burns its attacker.

A dragonfly does not look scary, either. But its flying skills are even more amazing than a dragon's. *Zoom!* This insect can fly forward, backward, in circles, and even upside-down. And it flies fast—35 miles per hour!

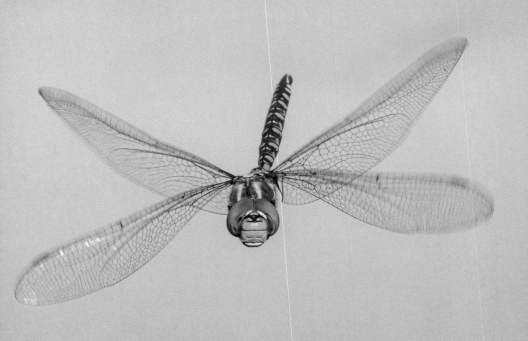

The pink dragon millipede is long and creepy. It also lives in caves like some dragons. But it is a bright pink bug! This bold coloring tells predators it is poisonous. *Pow!* Like the bombardier beetle, the pink dragon millipede releases chemical fire when threatened.

The blue dragon sea slug looks like a
tiny magical Chinese dragon. Instead
of scales, it has spines on its body called
cerata (say: suh-RAH-ta). *Zap!* The sea
slug stings a predator with the tips of its
cerata.

Finding Dragons

Many ideas about dragons came from "dragon bones" people found. We now know these bones were actually dinosaur fossils—the remains of extinct creatures from long ago found in rocks.

Pterosaurs (say: TERRA-sores) were the most like European dragons. They were giant reptiles with bat-like wings. They grew as tall as giraffes, had a wingspan of up to 40 feet, and could fly as fast as 80 miles per hour. Whoa!

41

Ancient people were said to have found and used dragon's blood to heal wounds. But it was likely the dark red sap from the rare dragon's blood tree.

Dragon's blood tree oil and resin

Today some scientists are studying the blood of Komodo dragons. They are looking for a way to treat new infections—called superbugs—that cannot be cured with medicines we have now. Dragons to the rescue!

Dragons were thought to be protectors. Statues of dragons were put in places that people wanted to guard. They can still be found on bridges, gates, town walls, and holy buildings.

On a famous pink temple in Thailand, a huge dragon curls around the outside of the tower. But it is not just for show— inside the dragon is a hidden staircase to the top!

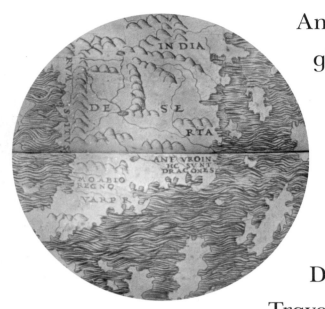 An ancient globe was marked with a warning message to explorers: "Here Be Dragons"! Travelers believed they had found dragons all around the world, but they probably saw giant lizards, reptiles, and snakes.

One place you can always find a dragon is in the night sky. The constellation—or cluster of stars—called Draco can be found close to the constellation Hercules. Hercules was once believed to be a Greek hero who defeated a mighty dragon.

Hercules constellation

47

The dragons of ancient tales may
never have existed. Or perhaps they were
once alive like dinosaurs, long ago. But
no matter what, dragons always live in
the hearts of those who are brave.
Do you believe?

OTHER LEVEL 4 BOOKS

*Penguin Young Readers are leveled by independent reviewers applying the standards developed by Irene Fountas and Gay Su Pinnell in *Matching Books to Readers: Using Leveled Books in Guided Reading*, Heinemann, 1999.

Are Dragons Real?

Did you know that people used to think dinosaur bones were actually dragon bones? Or that Alexander the Great claimed to have battled a dragon in India? Discover the history of this special creature, and decide for yourself if you believe in dragons!

LEVEL 1
Emergent Reader (F&P Text Levels A–D)

LEVEL 2
Progressing Reader (F&P Text Levels E–I)

LEVEL 3
Transitional Reader (F&P Text Levels J–M)

LEVEL 4
F&P TEXT LEVEL
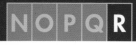
N O P Q R

Fluent Reader
- More advanced vocabulary
- Detailed and descriptive text
- Complex sentence structure
- In-depth plot and character development
- Full range of genres

*This book has been officially leveled by using the F&P Text Level Gradient™ leveling system.

ISBN 978-0-593-09316-0

EAN

5 0 4 9 9 >

9 780593 093160

$4.99 USA ($6.99 CAN)

PENGUIN YOUNG READERS
Visit us at penguinyoungreaders.com

Religion
#2

The Text and Contexts of Ignatius Loyola's "Autobiography"

John M. McManamon, S.J.